CONTENTS

INTRODUCTION

You've probably seen the commercials for the magical breakfast sandwich makers that, within five minutes or so, depending on the brand of sandwich maker, makes you a delicious breakfast sandwich that rivals the fast food joint with the golden arches. I hate making breakfast every morning, but I know how important it is and this gadget made it look so simple. So, my 12-year-old and I gave the breakfast sandwich maker a try.

How breakfast sandwich makers work
Using a breakfast sandwich maker is just as simple as the commercials make it look. You put a slice of bread in, add cheese and/or pre-cooked meat, slide the egg barrier in, crack an egg onto the egg barrier, top with another slice of bread and close.

Sandwiches in a snap
I tried the machine first and forgot to put the bread on top twice because I got distracted. This caused the egg to dribble out the side of the machine. No problem! The fantastic no-stick coating on the unit allowed me to wipe the egg off with one swipe of a towel. I was impressed.

Once I slowed down and used the machine like it was intended it was smooth sailing. The bread got properly toasted and the eggs cooked beautifully. My 12-year-old got the hang of using the sandwich maker on the first try.

I liked how the yolk stayed perfectly runny for those in our family that like runny yolks. For those that didn't like runny yolk, I simply scrambled the egg up with a fork a little bit after I dropped the egg in.

Timing is everything
What I didn't like is that there wasn't a reliable timer on the unit. It does have a preheat light, but as the manual says, this light doesn't indicate when the sandwich is done. Setting a kitchen timer to the suggested five minutes isn't a good remedy, either. We found that it can take anywhere from three to six minutes for a sandwich to cook, depending on the ingredients.

Eventually I found that it was best to just lift the lid up and take a peek every couple of minutes. This means you need to stick around and stay alert. It isn't an appliance you can set and leave to cook while you get ready for your day.

Don't smoosh

When using a panini maker, you may be used to squishing your sandwiches, but don't do that with a breakfast sandwich maker. Gently place the lid on top of your bread; it doesn't need to close completely to cook. If you do smoosh the lid down into place the egg with burst out of the appliance and will get all over your countertops.

Bread switch-up

All of the pictures on the box showed sandwiches made with round breads like bagels and English muffins, but we decided to give sliced loaf bread a try, too. You have to smash the edges of the bread into the unit just a bit, but it still came out perfectly toasted.

Cleaning up

Cleaning the breakfast sandwich maker is easy, too. Lifting the lid releases the sandwich making rings. They can be put in the dishwasher or can be washed by hand in hot, soapy water.

The plates on the unit can't be removed, but they can be wiped with a soapy sponge and then "rinsed" with a sponge damped with clean, warm water.

After you clean the unit, everything should be dried and coated with a non-stick cooking spray or wiped with vegetable oil to keep everything non-stick and tarnish-free.

CLASSIC BREAKFAST SANDWICH RECIPES

Everything Bagel Mushroom And Mozzarella Sandwich

Servings: 1
Cooking Time: 3 Minutes

Ingredients:

- 1 Everything Bagel
- 3 tbsp marinated Mushrooms
- 1 ½ ounce shredded Mozzarella Cheese
- 1 tsp Mustard
- 1 tsp chopped Parsely

Directions:

1. Preheat the sandwich maker and spray the inside of the unit with cooking spray.
2. Cut the bagel in half and lightly brush the insides with mustard.
3. When the green light appears, place one half of the bagel into the bottom ring, with the cut-side up.
4. Sprinkle the cheese over and top with the mushrooms and parsley.
5. Lower the cooking plate and top ring and add the second bagel half with the cut-side down.
6. Close and cook for 3 minutes.
7. Slide out the plate by rotating clockwise, open, and transfer to a plate.
8. Enjoy!

Nutrition:

- Info
- Calories 365 Total Fats 9.7g Carbs 52g Protein 17g Fiber 3.7g

Pizza Sandwich

Servings: 1
Cooking Time: 5minutes

Ingredients:

- 2 Bread slices, sourdough
- Butter
- 4 -5 Chicken strips (you can use pre-cooked)
- 1 tbsp. Marinara sauce
- 8 slices Pepperoni
- 2 slices Cheese, Mozzarella
- ½ tbsp. Parmesan cheese, grated

Directions:

1. Preheat the sandwich maker.
2. Spread butter on each bread slices.
3. On the side without butter layer the Ingredients: mozzarella, pepperoni, marinara sauce, chicken strips, and Parmesan.
4. Top with a slice of bread but place the butter side up.
5. Cook on the sandwich maker for about 5 minutes.
6. Serve and enjoy!

Tropical Croissant With Sugar

Servings: 1
Cooking Time: 4 Minutes

Ingredients:
- 1 tbsp mashed canned Pineapple
- 1 tbsp Mango chunks
- 1 tsp Butter
- ½ Croissant
- 1 tsp Powdered Sugar

Directions:
1. Preheat the unit and grease it with cooking spray.
2. Spread the butter over the croissant, and place on top of the bottom ring, with the butter-side down.
3. Top with the pineapple and mango chunks.
4. Close the lid and cook for 3 minutes.
5. Rotate clockwise, and lift to open carefully.
6. Transfer to a plate and sprinkle with the powdered sugar.
7. Enjoy!

Nutrition:
- Info
- Calories 194 Total Fats 10g Carbs 24.6g Protein 2.6g Fiber 1.3g

Olive And Cheese Snack

Servings: 1
Cooking Time: 3 Minutes

Ingredients:
- 1 Bread Slice
- 1 ounce Shredded Cheese
- 1 Basil Leaf, chopped
- 2 Kalamata Olives, diced

Directions:
1. Grease the unit and preheat it until the green light appears.
2. Cut the bread slice so that it can fit inside the unit, and place it on top of the bottom ring.
3. Top with the olives, basil, and cheese.
4. Close the lid and cook for 3 minutes.
5. Rotate clockwise and open carefully.
6. Transfer with a non-metal spatula and enjoy!

Nutrition:
- Info
- Calories 205 Total Fats 12.7g Carbs 15g Protein 10g Fiber 2.1g

Eggs Benedict Sandwich

Servings: 1
Cooking Time: 4 To 5 Minutes

Ingredients:
- 4 Baby Spinach Leaves
- 1 English Muffin
- 1 Slice Canadian Bacon
- 1 tbsp Hollandaise Sauce
- 1 Egg, lightly whisked

Directions:
1. Preheat the Hamilton Beach Breakfast Sandwich Maker and spray it with some cooking spray.
2. Split the muffin in half and add one half to the bottom ring.
3. Top with the baby spinach and bacon.
4. Lower the cooking plate and add the egg to it.
5. Top with the remaining muffin half and close the unit.
6. Let cook for 4 to 5 minutes.
7. Turn the handle clockwise and open carefully.
8. Transfer the sandwich with a plastic spatula to a plate.
9. Drizzle the Hollandaise Sauce on top.
10. Enjoy!

Nutrition:
- Info
- Calories 330 Total Fats 14.7g Carbs 31g Protein 19g Fiber 2.5g

Maple Bacon Waffle Sandwich

Servings: 1
Cooking Time: 4 Minutes

Ingredients:

- 2 small round waffles (store bought or homemade)
- Maple syrup
- 2 strips maple bacon
- 1 slice cheddar cheese
- 1 egg
- 1 Tbsp. milk
- Sea salt and pepper

Directions:

1. Place one waffle in the bottom of sandwich maker. Drizzle some maple syrup on top, then the maple bacon and cheddar cheese.
2. Lower the cooking plate and top ring. In a small bowl, whisk together egg, milk, sea salt and pepper; pour into egg plate. Top with other waffle.
3. Close the cover and cook for 4 to 5 minutes or until egg is cooked through and cheese is melted. Slide the egg plate out and remove sandwich with a rubber spatula. Cut in half.

Vegan Pepper Jack Roasted Pepper Panini

Servings: 1
Cooking Time: 4 Minutes

Ingredients:
- 2 slices bread (sourdough used)
- 2 tsp. vegan buttery spread
- 5 thin slices of tomato
- 1/4 cup (handful) of fresh basil leaves
- 1/4 - 1/3 cup vegan pepper jack cheese shreds such as Daiya
- 2-3 thin slices roasted red or yellow pepper
- 1/2 cup baby spinach
- pinches of black pepper jacklespoon Harissa

Directions:
1. Spread what's going to be the outside of each piece of bread with the vegan buttery spread. Spread the Harissas on what's going to be the inside of each piece of bread.
2. Place the tomatoes on one of the pieces of bread, then the spinach, then the basil, then the peppers, and top with the vegan cheese. Place the other piece of bread on top with the Harissa touching the cheese.
3. Cook the Panini on medium heat for 2 to 4 minutes, flipping halfway through. The bread should be brown, and the cheese should be melted.

Sausage And Cheese

Servings: 1
Cooking Time: 5 Minutes

Ingredients:
- 1 buttermilk biscuit, sliced
- 1 maple pork sausage patty, cooked
- 1 slice cheddar cheese
- 1 large egg, beaten

Directions:
1. Preheat the breakfast sandwich maker.
2. Place half of the biscuit, cut-side up, inside the bottom tray of the sandwich maker.
3. Arrange the sausage patty on top of the biscuit and top with the slice of cheddar cheese.
4. Slide the egg tray into place and pour the beaten egg into it.
5. Top the egg with the other half of the biscuit.
6. Close the sandwich maker and cook for 4 to 5 minutes until the egg is cooked through.
7. Carefully rotate the egg tray out of the sandwich maker then open the sandwich maker and enjoy your sandwich.

Bacon Chipotle Chicken Panini

Servings: 1
Cooking Time: 5 Minutes

Ingredients:
- 2 slices sourdough bread
- 1/4 cup Caesar salad dressing
- 1 cooked chicken breast, diced
- 1/2 cup shredded Cheddar cheese
- 1 tablespoon bacon bits
- 1 1/2 teaspoons chipotle chili powder, or to taste
- 2 tablespoons softened butter

Directions:
1. Spread the salad dressing on one side of both pieces of bread. Then top the dressing side of one piece of bread with chicken, then cheese, then bacon, and finally chipotle chili powder. Place the other piece of bread with the dressing side down on top. Butter the other side of both pieces of bread.
2. Cook the Panini on medium heat for 5 minutes, flipping halfway through. The bread should be brown, and the cheese should be melted.

Bacon Egg And Sausage Breakfast Panini

Servings: 2

Cooking Time: 6 Minutes

Ingredients:
- 2 pita breads
- 1/2cup pesto
- 2 eggs
- 1 cup shredded sharp cheddar cheese
- 1 cup shredded Monterey Jack cheese
- 1 cup shredded mozzarella cheese
- 1 pork sausage patty, cooked
- 2 strips bacon, cooked
- 1/3 cup roasted red pepper
- 1-2 tablespoons butter, melted
- 2 scallions, chopped

Directions:
1. Use a whisk to beat the egg with a pinch of salt and pepper.   Place the butter in a skillet and melt it on medium heat. Use a spoon to stir the eggs and push them across the pan. Cook until the eggs set, about 1 to 2 minutes.
2. Chop the sausage into small pieces. Spread the pesto on half of both pieces of pita. Top the pitas with half the cheese, then eggs, bacon, sausage, bell pepper, the remaining, cheese and then top with the scallions. Fold the other side of the pita on top of the filling, and spread the butter on the outside of the pitas.
3. Cook the Panini on medium heat for 4 to 6 minutes, flipping halfway through. The bread should be brown, and the cheese should be melted.

Prosciutto And Fig Panini

Servings: 4
Cooking Time: 6 Minutes

Ingredients:
- 8 (0.9-ounce) slices crusty Chicago-style Italian bread
- 4 ounces very thinly sliced prosciutto
- 1 1/4 cups (4 ounces) shredded Fontina cheese
- 1/2 cup baby arugula leaves
- 1/4 cup fig preserves
- Olive oil

Directions:
1. Lightly coat the one side of each piece of bread with olive oil using a brush.
2. Spread the fig preserve on 4 pieces of bread (not on the olive oil side). On the other pieces of bread put a layer of prosciutto, then arugula and top with cheese. Place the fig coated bread on top with the fig side touching the cheese.
3. Cook the Panini on medium heat for 6 minutes, flipping halfway through. The bread should be brown, and the cheese should be melted.

Canned Salmon And Bacon Pickle Sandwich

Servings: 1
Cooking Time: 3-4 Minutes

Ingredients:
- 2 ounces canned Salmon
- 1 Bacon Slice, cooked
- 2 Bread Slices
- 1 ounce shredded Mozzarella Cheese
- 1 tsp Pickle Relish
- ½ Pickle, sliced
- 1 tsp Dijon Mustard
- 1 tsp Tomato Puree

Directions:
1. Preheat the sandwich maker and grease it with some cooking spray.
2. Cut the bread slices so they can fit the unit.
3. Brush one of the bread slices with Dijon mustard and place it on top oh the bottom ring, with the mustard-side up.
4. Add the salmon and bacon on top and sprinkle with the relish and tomato puree.
5. Arrange the pickle slices over and top with the mozzarella.
6. Lower the top ring and add the second bread slice.
7. Cover the unit and cook for about 3-4 minutes.
8. Rotate clockwise to open an transfer to a plate.
9. Serve and enjoy!

Nutrition:
- Info
- Calories 420 Total Fats 34g Carbs 25g Protein 28g Fiber 3.5g

Avocado Sandwich With Egg, Ham And Cheese

Servings: 1
Cooking Time: 4 Minutes

Ingredients:
- 4 Large Avocado Slices
- 1 Egg
- 1 Ham Slice
- 1 slice American Cheese
- Salt and Pepper, to taste

Directions:
1. Preheat the sandwich maker until the green light appears and grease it with cooking spray.
2. Arrange two of the avocado slices on the bottom ring.
3. Place the ham and cheese on top.
4. Lower the cooking plate and crack the egg into it. Season with salt and pepper.
5. Top with the remaining avocado slices.
6. Close the sandwich maker and cook for 4 minutes.
7. Side out and rotate clockwise. Open and transfer the sandwich with a spatula, very carefully, as you are using avocado slices, not bread.
8. Serve and enjoy!

Nutrition:
- Info
- Calories 580 Total Fats 44g Carbs 21g Protein 28g Fiber 12g

Banana Foster Sandwich

Servings: 8
Cooking Time: 10minutes

Ingredients:
- 4 oz. softened Cream Cheese
- 2 tbsp. of Brown sugar
- ½ cup Bananas, chopped
- 2 oz. Chocolate, chopped, Semi-Sweet
- 8 Bread slices, Italian bread
- 2 tbsp. melted butter

Directions:
1. Preheat the sandwich maker.
2. In a bowl combine the sugar and cream cheese. Blend until soft. Add the chocolate and bananas, mix again.
3. Spread on 4 Italian bread slices and cover with the other bread slices.
4. Brush sides with butter.
5. Grill for about 2 minutes.
6. Cut the sandwiches in half and serve.

Portabella And Spinach Croissant

Servings: 1
Cooking Time: 5 Minutes

Ingredients:
- 1 croissant, sliced
- 1 tsp. olive oil
- 1 cup baby spinach
- 1 tbsp. grated parmesan cheese
- 1 clove garlic, minced
- 1 portabella mushroom cap
- Salt and pepper to taste
- 1 large egg

Directions:
1. Heat the olive oil in a small skillet over medium heat. Stir in the garlic and cook for 1 minute.
2. Add the spinach and cook for 2 minutes, stirring, until just wilted. Remove from heat and stir in the parmesan cheese.
3. Preheat the breakfast sandwich maker.
4. Place half of the croissant, cut-side up, inside the bottom tray of the sandwich maker.
5. Top the croissant with the spinach mixture and the portabella mushroom cap. Sprinkle the mushroom with salt and pepper to taste.
6. Slide the egg tray into place and crack the egg into it. Use a fork to stir the egg, just breaking the yolk.
7. Place the second half of the croissant on top of the egg.
8. Close the sandwich maker and cook for 4 to 5 minutes until the egg is cooked through.
9. Carefully rotate the egg tray out of the sandwich maker then open the sandwich maker to enjoy your sandwich.

Masala Sandwich

Servings: 1
Cooking Time: 5minutes

Ingredients:
- 2 slices of sandwich Bread
- 1 cucumber, sliced
- Margarine
- 1/3 red onion, small, sliced
- 1 Tomato, ripe, sliced
- Chaat Masala to taste

Directions:
1. First, spread margarine on the bread slices
2. Layer the veggies, start with the cucumber, tomatoes and then onion.
3. Sprinkle with chat masala.
4. Close the sandwich and grill on the Panini maker. Grill for 3 minutes.
5. Serve immediately and enjoy!

Monte Cristo Sandwich

Servings: 1
Cooking Time: 5 Minutes

Ingredients:
- 2 slices frozen French toast
- 1 slice deli ham
- 1 slice provolone cheese
- 1 slice Swiss cheese
- 1 teaspoon maple syrup

Directions:
1. Preheat the breakfast sandwich maker.
2. Place one slice of French toast inside the bottom tray of the sandwich maker.
3. Arrange the slices of ham, provolone and Swiss cheese on top of the French toast slice.
4. Lower the ring on the top of the breakfast sandwich maker into place and place the other slice of French toast on top of the cheese.
5. Close the sandwich maker and cook for 4 to 5 minutes until the cheese is melted and the French toast heated through.
6. Carefully open the sandwich maker and drizzle the sandwich with maple syrup to enjoy.

Biscuit Sandwich

Servings: 2 - 4
Cooking Time: 15minutes

Ingredients:

- 4 eggs
- 4 eggs, the whites
- 2 tbsp. cream
- ¼ tsp. of Garlic salt
- 6 Bacon Slices
- ¾ cup Cheddar cheese, shredded
- 4 biscuits, refrigerated

Directions:

1. In a bowl combine the egg whites, eggs, garlic salt, and cream. Whisk well and cook them until fluffy and light.
2. Cook the slices of bacon and then set aside. (You can prepare the first 2 steps ahead but keep them in the fridge until you are ready to prepare the sandwich.)
3. Spray the press with cooking oil and layer with half biscuits. Top with ¼ eggs, bacon, 2 tbsp. cheese and top with the other biscuit.
4. Cook for 5 minutes and serve.

Bahn Mi Panini

Servings: 1
Cooking Time: 4 Minutes

Ingredients:
- 1 petite baguette roll or 7-inch section from a regular baguette
- Mayonnaise
- Maggi Seasoning sauce or light (regular) soy sauce
- Liver pâté, boldly flavored cooked pork, sliced and at room temperature
- 3 or 4 thin, seeded cucumber strips, preferably English
- 2 or 3 sprigs cilantro, coarsely chopped
- 3 or 4 thin slices jalapeno chili
- 1/4 cup Daikon and Carrot Pickle

Directions:
1. Cut the bread in half lengthwise. Use your fingers to take out some of the soft part of the middle of both pieces of bread.
2. Spread the mayonnaise inside both pieces of bread. Lightly coat with the Maggi seasoning sauce, then place the meat on top followed by the cucumbers, cilantro, jalapenos, and then pickles.
3. Cook the Panini on medium heat for 4 minutes, flipping halfway through. The bread should be nicely toasted.

Muffin Sandwich With Egg, Ham, And Cheese

Servings: 1

Cooking Time: 5 Minutes

Ingredients:

- 1 slice Cheese
- 1 English Muffin
- 1 slice Canadian Bacon
- 1 Egg, scrambled

Directions:

1. Preheat and grease the sandwich maker.
2. Cut the English muffin in half and place one half with the spilt-side up into the bottom ring.
3. Top with the bacon and cheese.
4. Now, lower the cooking plate and add the egg inside.
5. Close and let cook for 4-5 minutes.
6. Slide clockwise to open using mittens.
7. Remove the sandwich carefully and transfer to a plate.
8. Serve and enjoy!

Nutrition:

- Info
- Calories 357 Total Fats 17g Carbs 26g Protein 24g Fiber 2g

Yogurt And Dill Open Cod Sandwich

Servings: 1
Cooking Time: 3 Minutes

Ingredients:
- 1 small Pita Bread, about 4 inches
- 3 ounces cooked Cod, chopped
- 1 tbsp Greek Yogurt
- 1 tsp chopped Dill
- ¼ tsp Garlic Powder
- 1 ounce shredded Cheddar Cheese

Directions:
1. Preheat the unit until the green light appears. Grease with cooking spray.
2. Add the pita bread to the bottom ring and place the cod on top.
3. Sprinkle with the garlic powder and top with the cheddar.
4. Close the lid and cook for 3 minutes or so.
5. Combine the yogurt and dill.
6. Open the lid carefully and transfer to a plate.
7. Drizzle the yogurt and dill mixture over.
8. Enjoy!

Nutrition:
- Info
- Calories 282 Total Fats 12g Carbs 17g Protein 26.5g Fiber 0.6g

Lamb Panini With Mint And Chili Chutney

Servings: 4

Cooking Time: 55 Minutes

Ingredients:

- ¾ cup Chili Chutney
- 2 teaspoon fresh mint, finely chopped
- 1 teaspoon wholegrain mustard
- 2 tablespoons sour cream or cream cheese
- Salt and freshly ground black pepper
- 4 Panini rolls or olive Ciabatta rolls, cut in half
- 4-8 slices roast lamb
- ½ cup caramelized red onion
- ½ cup feta cheese, crumbled
- 1½ cup arugula

Directions:

1. Combine the chutney, mint, mustard, sour cream, and pepper. Allow it to rest for 15 minutes
2. Spread the chutney mixture on the inside part of both halves of the rolls. Brush the other side of the bread with olive oil. Put a layer of onions on the bottom half of the roll, then lamb, arugula, and then feta, and top with the other half of the roll.
3. Cook the sandwiches for 6 minutes on medium heat, and make sure to flip halfway through. The bread should be nicely toasted and the cheese should be melted.

Beans & Veggies Sandwich

Servings: 1
Cooking Time: 8 Minutes

Ingredients:

- 2 slices multigrain bread
- 2 Tbsp. canned black beans
- 2 tsp. diced green onion
- 2 tsp. shredded carrot
- 2 tsp. shredded radish
- 1 slice Pepper Jack cheese
- 1 egg
- Sea salt and pepper

Directions:

1. Spread black beans on both slices of bread. Place one slice, beans side up, into the bottom ring of sandwich maker. Sprinkle green onion, carrot and radish on top. Top with Pepper Jack cheese.
2. Lower the cooking plate and top ring; crack an egg into the egg plate and pierce to break the yolk. Season with sea salt and pepper. Top with other slice of bread.
3. Close the cover and cook for 4 to 5 minutes or until egg is cooked through. Gently slide the egg plate out and remove sandwich with a rubber spatula.

Bruschetta Turkey Panini

Servings: 4

Cooking Time: 4 Minutes

Ingredients:
- 8 slices Italian bread
- 8 fresh basil leaves
- 8 thinly sliced tomatoes
- 16 slices of Black Pepper Turkey Breast
- 4 pieces of mozzarella cheese
- 4 tablespoons mayonnaise
- Olive oil

Directions:
1. Cut the basil into ribbons.
2. Place a layer of turkey on a piece of bread, then basil, and then cheese. Spread the mayo on the bottom part of the top piece of bread, and place it on top of the cheese. Brush the top and bottom of the sandwich with olive oil
3. Cook the sandwiches for 4 minutes on medium heat, and make sure to flip halfway through. The bread should be brown, and the cheese should be melted.

Classic Italian Cold Cut Panini

Servings: 2
Cooking Time: 6 Minutes

Ingredients:
- 1 12 inch hoagie rolls or the bread of your choice
- 1 tablespoon olive oil
- 2 ounces Italian dressing
- 4 slices provolone cheese
- 4 slices mortadella
- 8 slices genoa salami
- 8 slices deli pepperoni
- 4 slices tomatoes
- 2 pepperoncini peppers, chopped

Directions:
1. Slice the rolls in half and then cut it open.
2. Lightly coat the outside of the roll with olive oil using a brush.
3. Brush the inside each piece of bread with the dressing. Then top the bottom pieces of bread with cheese. Add the mortadella, salami, tomatoes and pepperoncini's
4. Cook the Panini on medium heat for 6 minutes, flipping halfway through. The bread should be brown, and the cheese should be melted.

Ham-mango Croissant

Servings: 1
Cooking Time: 5 Minutes

Ingredients:

- 1 small croissant, sliced in half
- 1 slice ham
- A few slices mango
- Dash of cayenne pepper
- 1 slice white cheddar cheese
- 1 egg
- Sea salt and pepper

Directions:

1. Place one croissant half into the bottom ring of breakfast sandwich maker, cut side up. Place ham and mango on top, and lightly sprinkle with cayenne pepper. Next place the cheddar cheese.
2. Lower the cooking plate and top ring; crack an egg into the egg plate and pierce to break the yolk. Season with sea salt and pepper. Top with other croissant half.
3. Close the cover and cook for 4 to 5 minutes or until egg is cooked and sandwich is warmed through. Carefully remove sandwich with a rubber spatula.

Egg White Sandwich With Spinach And Goat's

Servings: 1
Cooking Time: 5 Minutes

Ingredients:
- 1 Whole Wheat English Muffin
- 2 Egg Whites
- 1 ounce Goat's Cheese
- 1 tbsp chopped Spinach
- 1 tbsp chopped Pepper
- Salt and Pepper, to taste

Directions:
1. Preheat and grease the sandwich maker.
2. Whisk the egg whites and season with some salt and pepper.
3. Cut the muffin in half.
4. Place one half in the bottom of the unit, with the cut-side up.
5. Top with the cheese, spinach, and pepper.
6. Lower the cooking plate and ring and pour the egg whites inside.
7. Top with the second half of the muffin, this time with the cut-side down.
8. Close the unit and cook for 5 minutes.
9. Rotate clockwise to open and transfer to a plate with a plastic or wooden spatula.
10. Serve and enjoy!

Nutrition:
- Info
- Calories 255 Total Fats 7.7g Carbs 29.5g Protein 19.5g Fiber 5.5g

Cheddar Hash Brown Biscuit

Servings: 1
Cooking Time: 5 Minutes

Ingredients:
- 1 buttermilk biscuit, sliced
- 1 frozen hash brown patty
- 1 slice cheddar cheese
- 1 large egg

Directions:
1. Heat the butter in a small skillet over medium heat. Add the hash brown patty and cook for 2 to 3 minutes until lightly browned on the underside.
2. Flip the patty and cook until browned on the other side. Remove from heat.
3. Preheat the breakfast sandwich maker.
4. Place half of the biscuit, cut-side up, inside the bottom tray of the sandwich maker.
5. Top the biscuit with the cooked hash brown patty and cheddar cheese slice.
6. Slide the egg tray into place and crack the egg into it. Use a fork to stir the egg, just breaking the yolk.
7. Place the second half of the biscuit on top of the egg.
8. Close the sandwich maker and cook for 4 to 5 minutes until the egg is cooked through.
9. Carefully rotate the egg tray out of the sandwich maker then open the sandwich maker to enjoy your sandwich.

Bacon & Green Chili Croissant

Servings: 1
Cooking Time: 5 Minutes

Ingredients:

- 1 medium croissant, sliced in half
- 2 tsp. mayonnaise
- 2 slices bacon
- 1 slice fresh tomato
- 1 – 2 tsp. canned diced green chilis
- 1 slice Swiss cheese
- Dash of chili powder
- 1 egg

Directions:

1. Spread mayonnaise on both halves of croissant. Place one half in the bottom of your breakfast sandwich maker, mayo side up. Place bacon, tomato, green chili and Swiss cheese on top. Sprinkle with a dash of chili powder.
2. Lower cooking plate and top ring. Crack an egg into the egg plate, piercing the yolk to break it. Top with other croissant half and cook for 4 – 5 minutes, or until egg is cooked through.
3. Gently slide the egg plate out and carefully remove sandwich with a rubber spatula.

Taleggio And Salami Panini With Spicy Fennel Honey

Servings: 6
Cooking Time: 10 Minutes

Ingredients:
- 1/3 cup honey
- 1 tablespoon fennel seeds
- 2 teaspoons chili flakes
- 1/2 loaf focaccia, cut into 4-inch squares
- 1 pound Taleggio, rind washed, room temperature, thinly sliced
- 12 slices fennel salami, thinly sliced

Directions:
1. Put the chili, fennel, and honey in a small saucepan and heat on medium heat. Allow the mixture to cook for 3 to 5 minutes.
2. Cut the focaccia in half horizontally. Layer the cheese on one piece of bread and layer the salami on top. Top the salami with a nice drizzle of the honey. Put the other piece of bread on top.
3. Brush the inside each piece of bread with the dressing. Then top the bottom pieces of bread with cheese. Add the mortadella, salami, tomatoes and pepperoncini's
4. Cook the Panini on medium-high heat for 10 minutes, flipping halfway through. The bread should be brown, and the cheese should be melted.
5. Top with more honey and serve warm.

Chipotle Chicken Sandwich

Servings: 1
Cooking Time: 5 Minutes

Ingredients:
- 1 ciabatta roll, sliced
- 1 cooked chicken patty
- 1 slice Pepper Jack cheese
- 1 tbsp. chipotle mayonnaise
- 1 large egg
- 1 slice red onion
- 1 piece romaine lettuce, torn in half

Directions:
1. Preheat the breakfast sandwich maker.
2. Place half of the ciabatta roll, cut-side up, inside the bottom tray of the sandwich maker.
3. Top the ciabatta with the chicken patty and Pepper Jack cheese.
4. Slide the egg tray into place and crack the egg into it. Use a fork to stir the egg, just breaking the yolk.
5. Brush the other half of the ciabatta roll with the chipotle mayonnaise.
6. Place the second half of the ciabatta on top of the egg.
7. Close the sandwich maker and cook for 4 to 5 minutes until the egg is cooked through.
8. Carefully rotate the egg tray out of the sandwich maker then open the sandwich maker.
9. Remove the top ciabatta roll and top the sandwich with the onion and lettuce. Replace the roll to enjoy the sandwich.

Chili Cheesy Omelet With Bacon

Servings: 1

Cooking Time: 4 ½ Minutes

Ingredients:

- 2 Eggs, whisked
- 1/4 Red Chili, chopped
- ¼ tsp Garlic Powder
- 1 slice cooked and crumbled Bacon
- 1 ounce Mozzarella Cheese, shredded
- Salt and Pepper, to taste

Directions:

1. Preheat and grease the sandwich maker.
2. Season the eggs with salt, pepper, and garlic powder.
3. When the green light appears, add half of the whisked eggs to the bottom ring.
4. Place the mozzarella, bacon, and chilli on top.
5. Add the remaining eggs to the cooking plate.
6. Close and let cook for 4 ½ minutes.
7. Open by sliding clockwise and transfer the omelet carefully to a plate.
8. Serve and enjoy!

Nutrition:

- Info
- Calories 277 Total Fats 18g Carbs 2.8g Protein 24.7g Fiber 2.8g

Ricotta Basil Biscuit With Nectarines

Servings: 1
Cooking Time: 5 Minutes

Ingredients:
- 1 buttermilk biscuit, sliced
- 1 ripe nectarine, peeled and sliced
- 1 tbsp. ricotta cheese
- 1 tbsp. maple syrup
- 2 tsp. brown sugar

Directions:
1. Place the nectarines in a bowl and add the ricotta, maple syrup and brown sugar then toss well.
2. Preheat the breakfast sandwich maker.
3. Place half of the biscuit, cut-side up, inside the bottom tray of the sandwich maker.
4. Top the muffin with the nectarine slices, ricotta, maple syrup and brown sugar mixture
5. Place the second half of the biscuit on top of the nectarines.
6. Close the sandwich maker and cook for 4 to 5 minutes until heated through.
7. Carefully open the sandwich maker and enjoy your sandwich.

Herbed Omelet With Cream Cheese And Cheddar

Servings: 1
Cooking Time: 4-5 Minutes

Ingredients:
- 1 ounce Shredded Cheddar
- 2 Eggs
- ¼ tsp Garlic Powder
- 2 tsp Cream Cheese
- 1 tsp chopped Parsley
- 1 tsp chopped Cilantro
- ½ tsp chopped Dill
- Pinch of Smoked Paprika
- Salt and Pepper, to taste

Directions:
1. Preheat and grease the sandwich maker.
2. Whisk the eggs and season with salt, pepper, garlic powder, and paprika.
3. Stir in the cream cheese, parsley, and cilantro.
4. When the green light appears, pour half of the eggs into the bottom ring of the unit.
5. Top with the shredded cheddar and dill.
6. Lower the top ring and cooking plate, and pour the remaining eggs inside.
7. Close the unit and let cook for 4 to 5 minutes.
8. Rotate the handle clockwise and transfer to a plate.
9. Serve as desired and enjoy!

Nutrition:
- Info
- Calories 290 Total Fats 22g Carbs 1.8g Protein 20.5g Fiber 0.1g

Cherry Chocolate Sandwich

Servings: 1
Cooking Time: 5minutes

Ingredients:

- 6 Cherry pieces, fresh, de - pitted and sliced
- 1 ½ tbsp. Chocolate spread
- 2 bread pieces
- 1 tsp. Olive oil

Directions:

1. Spread the chocolate on the bread. You can also use a different chocolate spread or a combo.
2. Wash and de – pit the cherries. Slice in half. Layer the cherries over the chocolate and top with the other half of the sandwich. Rub the outer side with olive oil.
3. Press on the sandwich maker for about 2 minutes per side.
4. Cut in half and serve. (It is better served when warm.)

Pork And Egg Tortilla Open Sandwich

Servings: 1
Cooking Time: 4 Minutes

Ingredients:

- 1 Wheat Tortilla
- 1 Egg
- 2 ounces cooked ground Pork
- 1 ounce shredded Cheddar Cheese
- 1 tbsp chopped Red Onion
- 1 tbsp Salsa

Directions:

1. Preheat and grease the sandwich maker.
2. Cut the tortilla, if needed, to fit inside the sandwich maker, and then add it to the bottom ring.
3. Place the pork on top of it, sprinkle the cheddar over, and top with the onion.
4. Lower the top ring and crack the egg into it.
5. Close the unit and wait for about 4 minutes before rotating the handle clockwise.
6. Open and transfer to a plate carefully.
7. Top with the salsa.
8. Enjoy!

Nutrition:

- Info
- Calories 466 Total Fats 28.3g   Carbs 20.5g Protein 31g Fiber 1.5g

Sweet And Salty Bacon Cheesy Panini

Servings: 4
Cooking Time: 3 Minutes

Ingredients:
- 8 oz. Brie, thinly sliced
- 8 pieces thick cut bacon, fully cooked
- 8 pieces Raisin-walnut bread
- ½ cup Apple butter
- Butter, softened

Directions:
1. Spread the apple butter on one side of each piece of bread. Then add 2 pieces of bacon to apple butter side of one piece of bread and top with ¼ of the cheese. Place another piece of bread on top with the apple butter side of the bread touching the cheese. Spread butter on the other side of both pieces of bread.
2. Cook the Panini on medium high heat for 2-3 minutes, flipping halfway through. The bread should be brown when ready.

Canadian Bacon & Provolone Bagel

Servings: 1
Cooking Time: 4 Minutes

Ingredients:
- 1 bagel, split
- 1 slice Canadian bacon
- 1 slice tomato
- 1 slice provolone cheese
- 1 egg
- Dash of Tabasco sauce

Directions:
1. Place one bagel half, cut side up into the bottom ring of breakfast sandwich maker. Place Canadian bacon, tomato and provolone cheese on top.
2. Lower the cooking plate and top ring; crack an egg into the egg plate and pierce to break the yolk. Sprinkle a few drops of Tabasco (to taste) on top. Top with other bagel half.
3. Close the cover and cook for 4 to 5 minutes or until egg is cooked through. Gently slide the egg plate out and remove sandwich with a rubber spatula.

Tilapia And Pimento Dijon Sandwich

Servings: 1
Cooking Time: 3-4 Minutes

Ingredients:
- 2 Bread Slices
- 2 ounces chopped cooked Tilapia Fillet
- 1 slice Pimento Cheese
- 2 tsp Dijon Mustard
- ¼ tsp chopped Parsley

Directions:
1. Preheat the sandwich maker and grease it with some cooking spray.
2. Cut the bread slices so they can fit inside the unit, and brush the Dijon over them.
3. Place one bread slice into the bottom ring, with the mustard-side up.
4. Add the tilapia, sprinkle with parsley, and top with cheese.
5. Lower the ring and add the second bread slice, with the mustard-side down.
6. Close the appliance and cook for 3 to 4 minutes.
7. Open carefully and transfer to a plate.
8. Serve and enjoy!

Nutrition:
- Info
- Calories 388 Total Fats 13g Carbs 35g Protein 29g Fiber 6g

Bacon Mozzarella, Zucchini And Tomato Panini

Servings: 4

Cooking Time: 8 Minutes

Ingredients:

- 6 slices bacon
- 1/2 large zucchini, cut lengthwise into 1/4" slices and grilled
- 3 tbsp. extra-virgin olive oil, divided
- kosher salt
- Freshly ground black pepper
- 1 medium yellow tomato, thinly sliced
- 1 medium red tomato, thinly sliced
- 1 loaf Ciabatta, halved lengthwise
- 8 oz. mozzarella, thinly sliced
- 2 tbsp. Freshly Chopped Basil

Directions:

1. Put the tomatoes on a plate lined with paper towel in order to soak up any excess liquid.
2. Use a brush to coat the inside of the bread with olive oil. Put down a layer of zucchini, then bacon, basil, and finally tomatoes. Salt and pepper to taste and top with top piece of bread. Use a brush to coat the top and bottom of sandwich.
3. Spread the butter on one side of each piece of bread. Place 2 pieces of bacon on the unbuttered side of a piece of bread, then 2 tomatoes and a ¼ of the cheese. Then top with the another piece of bread making sure the butter side is on top.
4. Cook the Panini on medium high heat for 6 to 8 minutes, flipping halfway through. The bread should be brown, and the cheese should be melted.

Gruyere, Apple And Ham Sandwich

Servings: 1
Cooking Time: 5 Minutes

Ingredients:

- 1 Ciabatta roll, sliced in half
- 1 slice ham
- A few apple slices
- 1 slice gruyere cheese
- 1 Tbsp. milk
- 2 tsp. diced onion
- 1 egg
- Sea salt and pepper

Directions:

1. Place one Ciabatta roll half into the bottom ring of breakfast sandwich maker. Place ham, apple slices and gruyere cheese on top.
2. In a small bowl whisk together milk, onion, egg, sea salt and pepper. Lower the cooking plate and top ring; pour egg mixture into egg plate. Top with other roll half.
3. Close the cover and cook for 4 to 5 minutes or until egg is cooked and cheese is melted. Remove sandwich with a rubber spatula.

Pepperoni Pizza Omelet

Servings: 1
Cooking Time: 4 Minutes

Ingredients:

- 2 Eggs
- 1 ounce Pepperoni, sliced
- 2 tsp Tomato Puree
- 1 ounces shredded Cheese
- Salt and Pepper, to taste

Directions:

1. Preheat and grease the sandwich maker.
2. Whisk the eggs in a bowl and season with some salt and pepper.
3. Stir in the tomato puree.
4. When the green light appears, pour half of the eggs to the bottom ring of the unit.
5. Top with the cheese and pepperoni.
6. Lower the cooking plate and the top ring, and pour the remaining eggs into the cooking plate.
7. Close and cook for 4 minutes.
8. Rotate the plate clockwise and transfer to a plate.
9. Serve and enjoy!

Nutrition:

- Info
- Calories 392 Total Fats 30g Carbs 3.2g Protein 25.6g Fiber 0.6g

Red Pepper And Goat Cheese Sandwich

Servings: 1
Cooking Time: 5 Minutes

Ingredients:
- 2 slices multigrain bread
- 1 ounce goat cheese
- 2 slices fresh red pepper
- 1 slice red onion
- Salt and pepper to taste
- 1 large egg

Directions:
1. Preheat the breakfast sandwich maker.
2. Place one slice of bread inside the bottom tray of the sandwich maker.
3. Top the bread with the goat cheese, red pepper and red onion. Season with salt and pepper to taste.
4. Slide the egg tray into place and crack the egg into it. Use a fork to stir the egg, just breaking the yolk.
5. Place the second slice of bread on top of the egg.
6. Close the sandwich maker and cook for 4 to 5 minutes until the egg is cooked through.
7. Carefully rotate the egg tray out of the sandwich maker then open the sandwich maker to enjoy your sandwich.

Huevos Rancheros On Tortilla

Servings: 1
Cooking Time: 4 Minutes

Ingredients:
- 1 Mini Wheat Tortilla
- 1 tsp chopped Red Pepper
- 1 Egg
- 2 tsp chopped Onion
- 1 tbsp Beans
- 2 tsp Salsa
- ¼ cup shredded Cheddar Cheese
- Salt and Pepper, to taste

Directions:
1. Preheat and grease the sandwich maker.
2. With a cookie cutter, cut out the tortilla if needed so it can fit inside the sandwich maker.
3. Whisk the egg in a bowl or directly in the cooking plate, and season with salt and pepper.
4. Stir in the onion and red pepper.
5. Place the tortilla into the bottom ring.
6. Place the beans and cheese on top.
7. Lower the cooking plate and pour the egg inside.
8. Close the unit and cook for 4 minutes.
9. Rotate clockwise to open and transfer to a plate, carefully, with a plastic spatula.
10. Top with the salsa.
11. Serve and enjoy!

Nutrition:
- Info
- Calories 360 Total Fats 21g Carbs 16g Protein 18g Fiber 2.5g

Sauerkraut Sandwich

Servings: 1
Cooking Time: 5minutes

Ingredients:
- 1 Hard roll, cut in half
- ½ cup Sauerkraut
- Sliced Bratwurst, cooked
- 2 oz. Swiss Cheese, shredded

Directions:
1. Cut the hard roll in half.
2. On one-half place the sauerkraut, bratwurst, and cheese. Place the second half of the roll.
3. Place on the sandwich maker and press for 5 minutes.
4. Serve and enjoy!

Raspberry Sandwich

Servings: 1
Cooking Time: 4minutes

Ingredients:
- 2 slices of Challah bread
- 2 tbsp. of Cream cheese
- ½ tbsp. Butter, melted
- 1 – 2 tbsp. Raspberry Preserves

Directions:
1. Turn on medium-high heat and preheat the sandwich maker.
2. Spread the cheese on one of the bread slices.
3. Spread the raspberry on the other bread slices.
4. Sandwich together and brush with butter.
5. Cook for 4 minutes.
6. Cut the sandwich in half and serve.

Sausage And Biscuit

Servings: 1
Cooking Time: 4 Minutes

Ingredients:
- 1 Frozen Beef Sausage Patty
- 1 Biscuit
- 1 tbsp Gravy
- 1 slice Cheese
- 1 Egg, lightly beaten
- Salt and Pepper

Directions:
1. Preheat the unit until the green light appears. Grease with cooking spray.
2. Cut the biscuit in half and place one on top of the bottom ring.
3. Add the patty and top with the cheese.
4. Lower the cooking plate and add the egg to it. Season with salt and pepper.
5. Close the lid and cook for at least 4 minutes.
6. Rotate clockwise and lift to open.
7. Transfer to a plate and drizzle the gravy over.
8. Serve and enjoy!

Nutrition:
- Info
- Calories 410 Total Fats 35g Carbs 21g Protein 29g Fiber 3g

Tuna And Corn Muffin Sandwich

Servings: 1
Cooking Time: 3 Minutes

Ingredients:
- 1 Whole Wheat English Muffin
- 2 ounces canned Tuna, drained
- 2 tsp Mayonnaise
- 2 tsp canned Corn
- 2 tsp chopped Tomatoes

Directions:
1. Preheat and grease the unit.
2. Cut the English muffin half.
3. When the green light appears, add half of the muffin to the bottom ring.
4. Combine together the tuna, mayonnaise, tomatoes, and corn.
5. Place the tuna mixture on top of the muffin half.
6. Lower the top ring and add the second half of the muffin.
7. Close the unit and cook for 3 minutes.
8. Rotate clockwise and open. Transfer to a plate.
9. Serve and enjoy!

Nutrition:
- Info
- Calories 255 Total Fats 9g Carbs 29.5g Protein 17g Fiber 5g

Spicy Soppressata Panini With Pesto And Mozzarella

Servings: 4

Cooking Time: 10 Minutes

Ingredients:

- 1 Ciabatta loaf, cut into 4 portions, or 4 Ciabatta rolls
- 1/2 cup basil pesto, purchased or homemade
- 8 ounces fresh mozzarella cheese, sliced
- 4 ounces sliced spicy Soppressata salami

Directions:

1. Cut the Ciabatta in half horizontally.
2. Spread the pesto on the inside of each piece of bread. Place a layer of salami on the bottom piece of bread and then place the cheese on top. Top with the other piece of bread
3. Cook the Panini on medium high heat for 5 to 7 minutes, flipping halfway through. The bread should be brown, and the cheese should be melted.

Bagel With Lox Sandwich

Servings: 1
Cooking Time: 5 Minutes

Ingredients:

- 1 whole grain bagel, sliced
- 2 ounces smoked salmon
- 2 tbsp. cream cheese
- 1 tsp. minced red onion
- 1 tsp. minced chives
- 1 large egg

Directions:

1. Preheat the breakfast sandwich maker.
2. Place one half of the bagel, cut-side up, inside the bottom tray of the sandwich maker.
3. Top the bagel with smoked salmon.
4. Stir together the cream cheese, red onion and chives then spread over the salmon.
5. Slide the egg tray into place and crack the egg into it. Use a fork to stir the egg, just breaking the yolk.
6. Place the second half of the bagel on top of the egg.
7. Close the sandwich maker and cook for 4 to 5 minutes until the egg is cooked through.
8. Carefully rotate the egg tray out of the sandwich maker then open the sandwich maker to enjoy your sandwich.

Cuban Sandwich

Servings: 2
Cooking Time: 10minutes

Ingredients:

- 2 soft sandwich rolls, slice them lengthwise
- Mustard
- 1 dill pickle, sliced lengthwise
- 4 oz. sliced roast turkey
- 4 oz. sliced ham
- 3 oz. Provolone or Swiss cheese
- Softened Butter

Directions:

1. Spread the rolls with mustard. Now layer ½ of the ingredients, cheese, ham, turkey and pickle on each roll. Press them together. Spread the outside with butter.
2. Grill using the Panini for 5 minutes.
3. Serve and enjoy!

Muffuletta Panini

Servings: 4

Cooking Time: 4 Minutes

Ingredients:
- softened butter
- 8 slices rustic bread or 8 slices sourdough bread
- 16 slices provolone cheese (thin slices) or 16 slices mozzarella cheese (thin slices)
- 1/2 cup olive salad, drained or 1/2 cup olive tapenade
- 6 ounces thinly sliced black forest ham
- 6 ounces sliced mortadella
- 4 ounces sliced genoa salami

Directions:
1. Spread butter on both sides of each piece of bread.
2. Place 2 pieces of cheese on 4 piece of bread. Then put down a layer of olive salad, ham, mortadella, salami and top with the remaining cheese. Then top with the another piece of bread
3. Cook the Panini on medium heat for 4 minutes, flipping halfway through. The bread should be brown, and the cheese should be melted.

Pesto Italian Bagel

Servings: 1
Cooking Time: 5 Minutes

Ingredients:
- 1 bagel, split
- 1 Tbsp. store bought pesto
- 1 slice ham
- 4 round slices pepperoni
- 1 slice tomato
- 1 slice provolone cheese
- 1 egg

Directions:
1. Spread pesto on both halves of bagel. Place one half, pesto side up into the bottom ring of breakfast sandwich maker. Place ham, pepperoni, tomato and provolone cheese on top.
2. Lower the cooking plate and top ring; crack an egg into the egg plate and pierce to break the yolk; top with other bagel half.
3. Close the cover and cook for 4 to 5 minutes or until egg is cooked through. Gently slide the egg plate out and remove sandwich with a rubber spatula.

Mexican-style Egg And Beans Sandwich

Servings: 1

Cooking Time: 5 Minutes

Ingredients:

- 2 slices whole wheat bread
- 1 ounce shredded Mexican cheese
- 2 tbsp. refried beans
- 1 large egg
- 1 tbsp. sliced green onion

Directions:

1. Preheat the breakfast sandwich maker.
2. Place one slice of bread inside the bottom tray of the sandwich maker.
3. Top the bread with the refried beans and cheese.
4. Slide the egg tray into place and crack the egg into it. Use a fork to stir the egg, just breaking the yolk.
5. Sprinkle the green onion over the egg then place the second piece of bread on top of the egg.
6. Close the sandwich maker and cook for 4 to 5 minutes until the egg is cooked through.
7. Carefully rotate the egg tray out of the sandwich maker then open the sandwich maker to enjoy your sandwich.

Chocolate Banana Croissant

Servings: 1
Cooking Time: 3 Minutes

Ingredients:
- 1 small croissant, sliced in half
- 1 Tbsp. chocolate hazelnut spread
- 3 – 4 slices of banana
- Shredded coconut

Directions:
1. Spread chocolate hazelnut spread on bottom half of croissant. Place in the bottom of breakfast sandwich maker. Place banana slices on top. Sprinkle with some shredded coconut.
2. Lower cooking plate and top ring. Place other half of croissant on top and close the sandwich maker lid. Cook for 2 – 3 minutes or until the croissant is warmed through. Carefully remove from sandwich maker. Enjoy immediately.

Chocolate Croissant

Servings: 1
Cooking Time: 3 Minutes

Ingredients:
- 2 ounces Chocolate, chopped
- 1 Croissant
- 1 tsp Heavy Cream

Directions:
1. Preheat the sandwich maker and grease it with some cooking spray.
2. Cut the croissant in half and place one half on top of the bottom ring, with the cut-side up.
3. Arrange the chocolate pieces on top and sprinkle with the heavy cream.
4. Lower the top ring and add the second croissant part, with the cut-side down.
5. Cook for 3 minutes.
6. Open carefully and transfer to a plate.
7. Serve and enjoy!

Nutrition:
- Info
- Calories 283 Total Fats 14g Carbs 32g Protein 6g Fiber 1.8g

Moist Leftover Chicken Biscuit

Servings: 1
Cooking Time: 4 Minutes

Ingredients:
- 1 Biscuit
- 2 ounces Leftover Chicken
- 2 tsp Heavy Cream
- 1 ounce shredded Cheddar Cheese

Directions:
1. Preheat the unit and grease it with cooking spray.
2. Cut the biscuit in half and add one half to the bottom ring, cut-side up.
3. Add the chicken and sprinkle the heavy cream over.
4. Top with the cheddar cheese and lower the top ring.
5. Add the second half of the biscuit, this time with the cut-side down, and close the unit.
6. Cook for 4 minutes.
7. Lift the lid and transfer the sandwich to a plate.
8. Serve and enjoy!

Nutrition:
- Info
- Calories 280 Total Fats 16g Carbs 12g Protein 22g Fiber 0.4g

Lamb And Havarti Grilled Cheese Panini

Servings: 1
Cooking Time: 8 Minutes

Ingredients:
- 2 slices thick hearty bread
- 1 tablespoon butter, room temperature
- 1/2 cup Havarti, shredded
- 1/4 cup leftover lamb, reheated
- sliced red onion
- handful of spinach
- 2 tablespoons tzatziki, room temperature

Directions:
1. Spread butter on one side of each piece of bread.
2. Place a layer of cheese down, then the lamb, spinach onions, and tzatziki on one piece of bread. Make sure it's not on the buttered side. Then top with the other piece of bread, making sure the buttered side is up.
3. Cook the sandwiches 8 minutes on medium heat, and make sure to flip halfway through. The bread should be brown, and the cheese should be melted.

Smoked Salmon And Brie Sandwich

Servings: 1
Cooking Time: 5 Minutes

Ingredients:

- 1 whole wheat English muffin, sliced
- 2 ounces smoked salmon
- 1 ounce Brie cheese, chopped
- 1 tbsp. chopped chives
- ½ tsp. chopped capers
- 1 large egg

Directions:

1. Preheat the breakfast sandwich maker.
2. Place half of the English muffin, cut-side up, inside the bottom tray of the sandwich maker.
3. Top the muffin with the salmon, chopped brie, chives and capers.
4. Slide the egg tray into place and crack the egg into it. Use a fork to stir the egg, just breaking the yolk.
5. Place the second half of the English muffin on top of the egg. Close the sandwich maker and cook for 4 to 5 minutes until the egg is cooked through
6. .Carefully rotate the egg tray out of the sandwich maker then open the sandwich maker to enjoy your sandwich

Ratatouille Panini

Servings: 1
Cooking Time: 16 Minutes

Ingredients:
- 1 red bell pepper, sliced
- 1 tomato, chopped
- 1 clove garlic, minced
- 1 teaspoon dried oregano, or to taste
- salt and ground black pepper to taste
- 1 eggplant, sliced
- 1 zucchini, sliced
- 1 tomato, sliced
- 1 red onion, sliced
- 4 teaspoons olive oil
- 4 slices sourdough bread
- 4 slices mozzarella cheese

Directions:
1. Warm a skillet on high heat, and place the red bell pepper in it for around 5 minutes. The pepper should be soft when it's ready. Place the red pepper, chopped tomato, garlic in a blender or food processor. Blend or process until a smooth sauce is formed. Add salt, pepper, and oregano to taste.
2. Grill the remaining vegetable on a grille or the same skillet for about 6 minutes flipping halfway through. The vegetables will be soft when ready.
3. Brush what's going to be the outside of the bread slices with olive oil. Spread the sauce on what's going to be the inside of the bread. Layer a piece of piece of cheese on 2 of the pieces of bread, then the vegetable mixture, then another piece of cheese. Top with another piece of bread with the sauce side touching the cheese.
4. Cook the Panini on medium heat for 4 to 5 minutes, flipping halfway through. The bread should be toasted, and the cheese should be melted.

Avocado Mash Sandwich

Servings: 1
Cooking Time: 8 Minutes

Ingredients:
- 2 slices French bread
- ½ small avocado
- 1 Tbsp. diced tomato
- ¼ tsp. garlic salt
- Black pepper
- 1 slice provolone cheese
- 1 egg

Directions:
1. Place one slice of French bread into the bottom ring of breakfast sandwich maker. In a small bowl, mash together avocado, tomato, garlic salt and pepper using a fork. Place avocado mixture on French bread slice and top with provolone cheese.
2. Lower the cooking plate and top ring; crack an egg into the egg plate and pierce to break the yolk. Top with other slice of French bread.
3. Close the cover and cook for 4 to 5 minutes or until egg is cooked through. Gently slide the egg plate out and remove sandwich with a rubber spatula.

The Ham & Cheese

Servings: 1
Cooking Time: 4 Minutes

Ingredients:
- 1 English muffin, split
- Grainy mustard
- 1 slice honey spiral ham
- 1 slice cheddar cheese
- 1 egg
- Red Hot sauce

Directions:
1. Spread some grainy mustard on both halves of English muffin. Place one half, mustard side up into the bottom ring of breakfast sandwich maker. Place ham and cheddar cheese on top.
2. Lower the cooking plate and top ring; crack an egg into the egg plate and pierce to break the yolk. Sprinkle a few drops of Red Hot sauce on the egg and top with other muffin half.
3. Close the cover and cook for 4 to 5 minutes or until egg is cooked through. Gently slide the egg plate out and remove sandwich with a rubber spatula.

Turkey Salsa Melt

Servings: 1
Cooking Time: 4 Minutes

Ingredients:

- 2 ounces leftover Turkey, chopped up nicely
- 1 English Muffin
- 1 tbsp Salsa
- 1 ounce shredded Cheese by choice
- 1 tsp chopped Celery

Directions:

1. Preheat and grease the sandwich maker.
2. Cut the muffin in half and place one half on top of the bottom ring, with the cut-size up.
3. Combine the turkey and salsa and place on top of the muffin.
4. Add the celery on top and sprinkle the cheese over.
5. Lower the top ring and add the second half with he cut-size down.
6. Close and cook for 4 minutes.
7. Carefully open the lid and transfer to a plate.
8. Serve and enjoy!

Nutrition:

- Info
- Calories 410 Total Fats 22g Carbs 21g Protein 20g Fiber 0.9g

Piña Colada Croissant

Servings: 1
Cooking Time: 4 Minutes

Ingredients:
- 1 small croissant, sliced in half
- 1 Tbsp. cream cheese
- 1 – 2 Tbsp. finely chopped pineapple
- Shredded coconut
- Honey

Directions:
1. Spread cream cheese on both croissant halves. Place one half into the bottom ring of breakfast sandwich maker, cut side up. Place chopped pineapple and shredded coconut on top. Drizzle with honey.
2. Lower the cooking plate and top ring; top with other croissant half. Close the cover and cook for 3 to 4 minutes or until sandwich is warmed through. Open sandwich maker and remove sandwich.

Classic Grilled Cheese Sandwich

Servings: 1
Cooking Time: 4 Minutes

Ingredients:

- 2 slices of Bread
- 1 ounce shredded Mozzarella
- 1 ounce shredded Gouda
- 2 tsp Butter

Directions:

1. Preheat the Hamilton Beach Breakfast Sandwich and grease it with some cooking spray.
2. Cut the bread slices so that they can fit inside the sandwich maker.
3. Spread 1 tsp of butter onto each of the slices.
4. Place one slice of the bread into the bottom ring with the butter-side down.
5. Top with the cheeses.
6. Lower the top ring and add the second slice, placing it with the butter-side up.
7. Close the appliance and cook for about 4 minutes, or less if you want it less crispy.
8. Slide out by rotating clockwise. Lift the cover carefully and transfer the sandwich to a plate.
9. Serve and enjoy!

Nutrition:

- Info
- Calories 453 Total Fats 25g Carbs 39g Protein 21g Fiber 6g

Easy Bread Pudding Sandwich

Servings: 1
Cooking Time: 5 Minutes

Ingredients:

- 2 slices stale bread, cubed
- 1 large egg
- 2 tbsp. maple syrup or honey
- 2 tbsp. plain yogurt
- 1 tbsp. melted butter
- Pinch ground nutmeg
- 1 chicken sausage patty, cooked
- 1 slice Swiss cheese
- 1 large egg

Directions:

1. Arrange the chunks of bread in a small round ramekin.
2. Whisk together the remaining ingredients and pour over the bread – do not stir.
3. Microwave the ramekin on high heat for 2 minutes until the pudding is firm and hot. Let cool for 5 minutes.
4. Preheat the breakfast sandwich maker.
5. Turn the bread pudding out of the ramekin and into the bottom of the breakfast sandwich maker.
6. Top the bread pudding with the sausage patty and slice of Swiss cheese.
7. Slide the egg tray into place and crack the egg into it. Use a fork to stir the egg, just breaking the yolk.
8. Close the sandwich maker and cook for 4 to 5 minutes until the egg is cooked through.
9. Carefully rotate the egg tray out of the sandwich maker then open the sandwich maker to enjoy your sandwich.

Ground Beef Sandwich Pitas

Servings: 8
Cooking Time: 10minutes

Ingredients:

- 2 ½ lb. Ground beef
- 1 onion, chopped
- ¾ cup Parsley, chopped
- 1 tbsp. Coriander, ground
- ¾ tsp. Cuminutes, ground
- ½ tsp. Cinnamon, ground
- 2 tsp. Salt
- 1 ½ tsp. Black pepper, ground
- ¼ cup of Olive oil
- 8 thick pita bread, medium, with pockets
- Olive oil to pat the pita bread.

Directions:

1. In a bowl add the ground beef and add ¼ cup of oil, black pepper, salt, cinnamon, cuminutes, coriander, parsley, and onion. Mix well and let it chill in the refrigerator for 1 hour.
2. Preheat the sandwich press on medium.
3. Open pockets in the bread and fill each with the ground mix. Try to fill it to the edges too. Press to seal.
4. Place them on the sandwich maker and cook for 5 minutes without applying too much pressure. Now press and cook for a few minutesutes more. Cook until the meat is cooked well.
5. Serve and enjoy!

Pear & Greens Sandwich

Servings: 1
Cooking Time: 5 Minutes

Ingredients:
- 1 biscuit, split
- 1 Tbsp. ricotta cheese
- Pear slices
- Piece of butter lettuce
- 1 Tbsp. finely chopped walnuts

Directions:
1. Spread ricotta cheese on both biscuit halves. Place one half into the bottom ring of breakfast sandwich maker, cheese side up. Place pear slices, butter lettuce and walnuts on top.
2. Lower the cooking plate and top ring; top with other biscuit half. Close the cover and cook for 3 to 4 minutes or until sandwich is warm. Remove with a rubber spatula and enjoy!

Monte-cristo With A Twist

Servings: 1
Cooking Time: 3 Minutes

Ingredients:
- 2 slices French or sour dough bread
- Butter
- Grape jelly
- 1 slice ham
- 1 slice provolone cheese
- 1 egg
- Powdered sugar

Directions:
1. Butter the outside of each slice of bread. Spread grape jelly on the inside of both slices. Place one slice into the bottom ring of breakfast sandwich maker, jelly side up. Place ham and provolone cheese on top.
2. Lower the cooking plate and top ring; crack an egg into the egg plate and pierce to break the yolk. Top with other slice of bread.
3. Close the cover and cook for 4 to 5 minutes or until egg is cooked through. Gently slide the egg plate out and remove sandwich with a rubber spatula. Dust with powdered sugar and serve.

Corned Beef And Cabbage Panini

Servings: 2

Cooking Time: 8 Minutes

Ingredients:
- 1 cup thinly sliced green cabbage
- 1 Tablespoons. olive oil
- ¼ teaspoon. table salt
- Freshly ground black pepper
- 1 teaspoon. yellow mustard seeds
- 2 Tablespoons. unsalted butter, softened
- 4 1/2-inch-thick slices rye bread with caraway seeds
- 1 Tablespoons. grainy mustard, more to taste
- 12 thin slices (6 oz.) corned beef
- 6 thin slices (3 oz.) Muenster cheese
- ¼ cup water

Directions:
1. Mix the water, cabbage, olive oil, mustard seeds, salt, and pepper in a saucepan, heat on medium-high heat until water boils. Once boiling lower heat to medium-low heat, cover, allow the mixture to cook for 10 to 15 minutes, stirring every once in a while. Remove the cabbage from the saucepan, and set aside any remaining water in the pan.
2. Butter one side of each piece of bread and place mustard on the other side. Top two pieces of bread, mustard side up with corned beef, then cabbage, and finally cheese. Top with the remaining pieces of bread, butter side up.
3. Cook the sandwiches for 6 to 8 minutes on medium heat, and make sure to flip halfway through. The bread should be brown, and the cheese should be melted.

Cheddar And Bacon Omelet

Servings: 1
Cooking Time: 3-4 Minutes

Ingredients:

- 2 Large Eggs
- 2 tbsp cooked and crumbled Bacon
- 2 tbsp shredded Cheddar Cheese
- Salt and Pepper, to taste

Directions:

1. Preheat your Breakfast Sandwich Maker and grease it with some cooking spray.
2. Beat the eggs lightly.
3. When the green lights turn on, open the unit, and add half of the whisked eggs into the bottom ring.
4. Top with the cheese and bacon.
5. Add the rest of the eggs to the cooking plate.
6. Close and cook for 3 to 4 minutes.
7. Rotate the handle clockwise to open.
8. Remove with a plastic or silicone spatula.
9. Serve and enjoy!

Nutrition:

- Info
- Calories 348 Total Fats 26g Carbs 1.2 g Protein 24.5g Fiber 0g

Pizza Snack

Servings: 1
Cooking Time: 4 Minutes

Ingredients:
- ½ English Muffin
- 4 mini Pepeproni Slices
- 1 tbsp shredded Cheddar Cheese
- 1 tsp Ketchup

Directions:
1. Preheat the unit until the green light appears and grease it with cooking spray.
2. Add the muffin to the bottom ring.
3. Spread the ketchup over it and top with the pepperoni and cheese.
4. Close the lid and cook for 3 minutes.
5. Open carefully and transfer to a plate with a non-metal spatula.
6. Serve and enjoy!

Nutrition:
- Info
- Calories 197 Total Fats 11.7g Carbs 14g Protein 8.5g Fiber 1g

The Ultimate Chicken, Spinach And Mozzarella Sandwich

Servings: 1
Cooking Time: 4 Minutes

Ingredients:

- 1 small Hamburger Bun
- 3 ounces cooked and chopped Chicken
- 1 tbsp Cream Cheese
- 1 ounce shredded Mozzarella
- 1 tbsp canned Corn
- 2 tbsp chopped Spinach

Directions:

1. Preheat and grease the sandwich maker.
2. Cut the bun in half and brush the cream cheese on the insides.
3. Add one half to the bottom ring, with the cut-side up.
4. Place the chicken on top and top with the spinach, corn, and mozzarella.
5. Lower the top ring and add the second half of the bun, the cut-side down.
6. Cook for 4 minutes.
7. Rotate clockwise and lift to open.
8. Serve and enjoy!

Nutrition:

- Info
- Calories 402 Total Fats 15.5g Carbs 32g Protein 32.5g Fiber 1.4g

Chocolate Hazelnut French Toast Panini

Servings: 4

Cooking Time: 6 Minutes

Ingredients:
- 6 large eggs
- 1 cup whole milk
- 1/2 cup heavy cream
- 1/4 cup fresh orange juice (from about 1 medium orange)
- 2 tablespoons vanilla extract
- 2 tablespoons cognac (optional)
- 2 tablespoons granulated sugar
- 1/2 teaspoon ground cinnamon
- Pinch of freshly grated nutmeg
- Salt
- 8 slices Texas toast or other thick white bread
- ½ cup hazelnut spread with cocoa
- ¼ cup chopped hazelnuts, toasted
- Confectioners' sugar, for garnish
- Pure maple syrup, for garnish

Directions:
1. Spread the hazelnut spread on 4 of the pieces of bread and then place the hazelnuts on top. Top with the pieces of bread.
2. Use a whisk to combine the eggs, milk, cream, orange juice, cognac, sugar, cinnamon, and vanilla. Put the sandwiches in a shallow baking dishes and cover with the mixture you just created. Allow the sandwiches to rest in the mixture for 10 minutes
3. Preheat your flip sandwich maker on medium high heat.
4. Cook the Panini for 6 to 7 minutes in your preheated flap sandwiched maker, flipping halfway through.
5. Top with confectioners' sugar and maple syrup

Portabella Havarti Melt

Servings: 1
Cooking Time: 4 Minutes

Ingredients:

- 2 slices crusty white bread
- 2 tsp. mayonnaise
- 1 tsp. Dijon mustard
- 1 portabella mushroom cap
- Spinach leaves
- 1 slice dill havarti cheese
- 1 egg

Directions:

1. Spread mayonnaise and Dijon mustard on both slices of bread. Place one slice, mayo side up into the bottom ring of breakfast sandwich maker. Place portabella mushroom, spinach leaves and havarti cheese on top.
2. Lower the cooking plate and top ring; crack an egg into the egg plate and pierce to break the yolk. Top with other slice of bread.
3. Close the cover and cook for 4 to 5 minutes or until egg is cooked through. Gently slide the egg plate out and remove sandwich with a rubber spatula.

Eggs Benedict With Ham

Servings: 1
Cooking Time: 5 Minutes

Ingredients:
- 4 tablespoons unsalted butter
- 1 large egg yolk
- 2 teaspoons lemon juice
- Pinch cayenne pepper
- Pinch salt
- 1 whole wheat bagel, sliced
- ½ cup fresh spinach leaves
- 2 slices cooked bacon
- 1 large egg, beaten

Directions:
1. Preheat the breakfast sandwich maker.
2. Melt the butter in a small saucepan over medium heat.
3. Blend the egg yolks, lemon juice, cayenne and salt in a blender then drizzle into the saucepan.
4. Cook for 10 seconds, stirring well, then remove from heat and set aside.
5. Place half of the bagel, cut-side up, inside the bottom tray of the sandwich maker.
6. Top the bagel half with spinach leaves. Break the bacon slices in half and place them on top of the spinach.
7. Slide the egg tray into place and pour the beaten egg into it.
8. Top the egg with the other half of the bagel.
9. Close the sandwich maker and cook for 4 to 5 minutes until the egg is cooked through.
10. Carefully rotate the egg tray out of the sandwich maker then open the sandwich maker.
11. Take the top bagel off the sandwich and drizzle the eggs with the hollandaise sauce.
12. Replace the bagel half and enjoy your sandwich.

Crunchy Nutella And Strawberry Bagel

Servings: 1
Cooking Time: 3 Minutes

Ingredients:
- ½ Bagel
- 1 tbsp Nutella
- 4 Strawberries, sliced
- 1 tsp chopped Hazelnuts

Directions:
1. Preheat the Hamilton Beach Breakfast Sandwich Maker until the green light appears. Spray with some cooking spray.
2. Spread the Nutella over the bagel.
3. Place the bagel on top of the bottom ring, with the cut-side up.
4. Arrange the strawberry slices over, and sprinkle with the hazelnuts.
5. Close the lid and cook for 3 minutes.
6. Rotate the handle clockwise to open.
7. Serve and enjoy!

Nutrition:
- Info
- Calories 220 Total Fats 8g Carbs 32g Protein 5.8g Fiber 2.2g

Thai Breakfast Sandwich

Servings: 1
Cooking Time: 6 Minutes

Ingredients:

- 2 slices whole wheat bread
- 1 Tbsp. peanut butter
- 1 Tbsp. shredded carrots
- 1 Tbsp. bean sprouts
- 1 tsp. finely chopped cilantro
- Dash of lime juice
- Dash of soy sauce
- 1 Tbsp. milk
- 1 egg
- Sea salt and pepper

Directions:

1. Spread peanut butter on both slices of bread. Place one slice into the bottom ring of breakfast sandwich maker, peanut butter side up. Pile the carrots, bean sprouts and cilantro on top. Sprinkle with lime juice and soy sauce.
2. In a small bowl whisk together milk, egg, sea salt and pepper. Lower the cooking plate and top ring; pour egg mixture in. Top with other slice of bread.
3. Close the cover and cook for 4 to 5 minutes or until egg is cooked. Remove sandwich with a rubber spatula.

Mediterranean Sandwich

Servings: 4
Cooking Time: 20minutes

Ingredients:

- 4 rolls, ciabatta, split
- 4 oz. Feta cheese, crumbled
- 24 oz. spaghetti or marinara sauce, divided
- 7 ½ oz. artichoke hearts, marinated, quartered and then chopped
- 2 Tomatoes, sliced
- 1 lb. Deli Turkey sliced thinly

Directions:

1. Spread 2 tbsp. marinara sauce on 4 roll halves.
2. Top the halves with cheese, turkey, tomato artichokes and again cheese. Spread 2 tbsp. Sauce and place the turkey. Top with the second roll hales.
3. Cook on the sandwich maker for 5 minutes.
4. Serve and enjoy!

Blta (bacon, Lettuce, Tomato And Avocado)

Servings: 1
Cooking Time: 5 Minutes

Ingredients:

- 1 croissant, sliced in half
- 1 tablespoon mayonnaise
- Salt and pepper to taste
- 3 slices bacon, cooked
- ¼ ripe avocado, pitted and sliced
- 1 thick slice tomato
- 1 piece Romaine lettuce, torn in half
- 1 large egg

Directions:

1. Preheat the breakfast sandwich maker.
2. Place half of the croissant, cut-side up, inside the bottom tray of the sandwich maker.
3. Brush the croissant with the mayonnaise and sprinkle with salt and pepper.
4. Break the bacon slices in half and arrange them on top of the croissant. Top with avocado and tomato.
5. Slide the egg tray into place and crack the egg into it. Use a fork to stir the egg, just breaking the yolk.
6. Place the second half of the croissant on top of the egg.
7. Close the sandwich maker and cook for 4 to 5 minutes until the egg is cooked through.
8. Carefully rotate the egg tray out of the sandwich maker then open the sandwich maker.
9. Remove the top of the croissant and top with the lettuce.
10. Replace the top half of the croissant then enjoy your sandwich.

Peanut Butter Waffle With Banana

Servings: 1
Cooking Time: 4 Minutes

Ingredients:
- 1 Frozen Waffle
- 1 tbsp Peanut Butter
- ¼ Banana, sliced

Directions:
1. Preheat the sandwich maker and grease it with some cooking spray.
2. Place the waffle on top of the bottom ring.
3. Spread the peanut butter over and close the lid.
4. Cook for about 3 minutes.
5. Open carefully and transfer to a plate.
6. Top with the banana slices and enjoy!

Nutrition:
- Info
- Calories 214 Total Fats 11g Carbs 25g Protein 6.3g Fiber 2.9g

Veggie Pepper Jack Sandwich With Arugula

Servings: 1
Cooking Time: 4 Minutes

Ingredients:

- 1 multigrain English muffin, split
- Sliced onion, bell pepper and radish
- A few arugula leaves
- 1 slice Pepper Jack cheese
- 1 egg

Directions:

1. Place one English muffin half, cut side up into the bottom ring of breakfast sandwich maker. Place slices of onion, bell pepper, radish, arugula leaves and Pepper Jack cheese on top.
2. Lower the cooking plate and top ring; crack an egg into the egg plate and pierce to break the yolk. Top with other muffin half.
3. Close the cover and cook for 4 to 5 minutes or until egg is cooked through. Gently slide the egg plate out and remove sandwich with a rubber spatula.

Tomato-basil With Mozzarella Sandwich

Servings: 1

Cooking Time: 5 Minutes

Ingredients:

- 2 slices specialty bread such as focaccia or sour dough
- 2 slices tomato
- A few fresh basil leaves
- 1 – 2 slices fresh mozzarella
- A few drops of balsamic vinegar
- 1 egg
- Sea salt and pepper

Directions:

1. Place one slice of bread into the bottom ring of breakfast sandwich maker. Place tomatoes, basil and mozzarella cheese on top. Sprinkle with balsamic vinegar.
2. Lower the cooking plate and top ring; crack an egg into the egg plate and pierce to break the yolk. Sprinkle with sea salt and pepper and top with other slice of bread.
3. Close the cover and cook for 4 to 5 minutes or until egg is cooked through. Gently slide the egg plate out and remove sandwich with a rubber spatula. Slice in half and enjoy!

Caribbean Sandwich

Servings: 1
Cooking Time: 5minutes

Ingredients:

- 2 slices of bread
- 1 tbsp. Yellow mustard
- Hot sauce to taste
- 3 slices queso Blanco
- 3 slices deli ham
- Fried or sautéed plantains
- Charred onion, red

Directions:

1. Spread the mustard on one bread slice.
2. Layer the remaining ingredients.
3. Add more queso Blanco to taste.
4. Place the second bread slice on top.
5. Press with the sandwich maker and cook for 5 minutes.
6. Serve and enjoy!

Salmon And Pistachio Melt

Servings: 1
Cooking Time: 3-4 Minutes

Ingredients:
- 2 Bread Slices
- 2 ounces chopped cooked Salmon
- 2 tsp chopped Pistachios
- 1 ounce shredded Mozzarella

Directions:
1. Preheat and grease the sandwich maker with cooking spray.
2. Cut the bread slices into circles so they can fit perfectly inside the unit.
3. Add the first slice to the bottom ring and place the salmon on top.
4. Add the pistachios over and top with the mozzarella.
5. Lower the top ring and add the remaining bread slice.
6. Close and cook for 3-4 minutes.
7. Rotate clockwise and lift open.
8. Transfer to a plate and enjoy!

Nutrition:
- Info
- Calories 423 Total Fats 16g Carbs 41g   Protein 30.8g Fiber 7g

Spicy Chocolate Hazelnut Bacon French Toast Panini

Servings: 4

Cooking Time: 6 Minutes

Ingredients:
- 6 large eggs
- 1 cup whole milk
- 1/2 cup heavy cream
- 1/4 cup fresh orange juice (from about 1 medium orange)
- 2 tablespoons vanilla extract
- 2 tablespoons cognac (optional)
- 2 tablespoons granulated sugar
- 1/2 teaspoon ground cinnamon
- Pinch of freshly grated nutmeg
- Salt
- Cayenne Pepper
- 8 strips of bacon, cooked
- 8 slices Texas toast or other thick white bread
- ½ cup hazelnut spread with cocoa
- ¼ cup chopped hazelnuts, toasted
- Confectioners' sugar, for garnish
- Pure maple syrup, for garnish

Directions:
1. Spread the hazelnut spread on 4 of the pieces of bread and then place the bacon on top. Add cayenne pepper to taste. Top with the pieces of bread.
2. Use a whisk to combine the eggs, milk, cream, orange juice, cognac, sugar, cinnamon, and vanilla. Put the sandwiches in a shallow baking dishes and cover with the mixture you just created. Allow the sandwiches to rest in the mixture for 10 minutes
3. Preheat your flip sandwich maker on medium high heat.
4. Cook the Panini for 6 to 7 minutes in your preheated flap sandwiched maker, flipping halfway through.
5. Top with confectioners' sugar and maple syrup

Spicy Turkey And Sausage Sandwich

Servings: 1
Cooking Time: 4 Minutes

Ingredients:
- 1 ounce cooked ground Turkey
- 4 slices of Spicy Sausage
- 2 tsp Salsa
- ¼ tsp Cumin
- 1 tbsp refined Beans
- 1 tsp Sour Cream
- 1 tbsp shredded Cheddar Cheese
- 2 small Tortillas

Directions:
1. Preheat the sandwich maker and grease it with some cooking spray.
2. Cut the tortillas into circles so they can fit inside the unit.
3. Add one tortilla on top of the bottom ring and spread half of the salsa over.
4. Top with the turkey and sausage, and sprinkle the cumin over.
5. Add the beans and cheese, and drizzle the sour cream over.
6. Brush the remaining salsa on the second tortilla and place it on top of the cheese with the salsa-side down.
7. Close the unit and cook for 4 minutes.
8. Lift it open and transfer to a plate carefully.
9. Serve and enjoy!

Nutrition:
- Info
- Calories 470 Total Fats 26g Carbs 32g Protein 26g Fiber 3g

Cheddar-apple Smoked Bacon Sandwich

Servings: 1
Cooking Time: 4 Minutes

Ingredients:

- 1 English muffin, split
- 1 tsp. grainy mustard
- 2 slices smoked bacon
- 3 thin apple slices
- 1 slice cheddar cheese
- 1 egg

Directions:

1. Spread the mustard on one half of the English muffin. Place muffin, mustard side up, into the bottom ring of breakfast sandwich maker. Place smoked bacon, apple slices and cheddar cheese on top.
2. Lower the cooking plate and top ring; crack an egg into the egg plate and pierce to break the yolk; top with other English muffin half.
3. Close the cover and cook for 4 to 5 minutes or until egg is cooked through. Gently slide the egg plate out and remove sandwich with a rubber spatula.

Peanut Butter Banana Sandwich

Servings: 1
Cooking Time: 5 Minutes

Ingredients:

- 2 slices white bread
- 2 tbsp. smooth peanut butter
- 1 large banana, sliced

Directions:

1. Preheat the breakfast sandwich maker.
2. Place one slice of bread, already coated with peanut butter, side up inside the bottom tray of the sandwich maker.
3. Top the bread with slices of banana.
4. Place the second piece of bread on top of the banana.
5. Close the sandwich maker and cook for 4 to 5 minutes until heated through.
6. Carefully open the sandwich maker and enjoy your sandwich.

Chicken, Avocado And Swiss Croissant

Servings: 1
Cooking Time: 5 Minutes

Ingredients:

- 1 small croissant, sliced in half
- 1 Tbsp. herb and chive cream cheese
- Strips of precooked chicken breast
- Avocado slices
- Sea salt and pepper
- 1 slice Swiss cheese
- 1 egg

Directions:

1. Spread the cream cheese on both halves of croissant. Place one half, cut side up into the bottom ring of breakfast sandwich maker. Place chicken breast and avocado on top; sprinkle with sea salt and pepper. Top with Swiss cheese.
2. Lower the cooking plate and top ring; crack the egg into the egg plate and pierce to break the yolk. Top with other croissant half.
3. Close the cover and cook for 4 to 5 minutes or until egg is cooked through. Slide the egg plate out by turning clockwise and remove sandwich with a rubber spatula.

Apple, Turkey And Cheddar Sandwich

Servings: 2

Cooking Time: 5minutes

Ingredients:
- 4 slices of Bread
- 4 tbsp. Butter
- 2 tbsp. Mustard
- 1 Apple, sliced thinly (green)
- 8 slices of Cheddar cheese, sharp
- 8 slices of deli turkey, roasted

Directions:
1. Preheat the sandwich press.
2. Spread 1 tbsp. butter on each bread slice.
3. Spread mustard on 2 bread slices. Lay the turkey, cheese and apple slices. Top with on bread slice.
4. Grill for about 5 minutes.
5. Let it rest for 1 minutes and serve.

RECIPES INDEX

T

Taleggio And Salami Panini With Spicy Fennel Honey 37

Thai Breakfast Sandwich 85

The Ham & Cheese 69

The Ultimate Chicken, Spinach And Mozzarella Sandwich 80

Tilapia And Pimento Dijon Sandwich 46

Tomato-basil With Mozzarella Sandwich 90

Tropical Croissant With Sugar 10

Tuna And Corn Muffin Sandwich 55

Turkey Salsa Melt 70

V

Vegan Pepper Jack Roasted Pepper Panini 14

Veggie Pepper Jack Sandwich With Arugula 89

Y

Yogurt And Dill Open Cod Sandwich 28

Printed in the USA
CPSIA information can be obtained
at www.ICGtesting.com
LVHW081735030124
768075LV00014B/935